February

Tatenda Munzara

BookLeaf Publishing

Presentation by *BookLeaf Publishing*

Web: www.bookleafpub.com

E-mail: info@bookleafpub.com

ISBN: 9789357744287

First edition 2023

*This is for every friend who has ever told
me I was brilliant and that my work,
passion, and talent is worth pursuing.
Thank you, Steph, for encouraging me to be
brave enough to share my poetry.*

ACKNOWLEDGEMENT

Thank you - to every teacher who believed in me and my ability, notably the drama department at The Langley Academy, the institutions that granted me the 'yes' and or 'approved', I needed in that season. To the friends that prayed for the protection and prosperity of my future, and the family members that have shown me, unconditional love and support. Finally, thank you, God, for the gift of storytelling..

PREFACE

The dream to be a published writer was locked away in the cellar where the wildest fantasies of make-believe existed. I thank God that poetry came into my life as the emancipator for those dreams. I truly thought I'd have to wait years and years to feel deserving to have my work printed and read by people. This poetry book is a mixture of the different pages of my story. I spent a month creating a narrative that could explore my personal journey of gaining self-confidence, whilst seeking professional help to unlearn habits and proactively move forward from traumatic life events. Reflecting on my first serious relationship, and the feelings attached to being ready for the next one. Lastly, holding space to celebrate the power of the community I'd built over the years whilst simultaneously feeling a sense of loneliness. This is February.

Ripped Jean Pocket

When I think about the affection my father gives
me, I imagine a passport-sized picture of myself
being placed in the ripped back pocket of his
jeans, loose thread and fabric waving around
like a dog's tongue.

Initiating hugs is the equivalent of eating
pineapple on pizza, the aim is to get through as
quickly as possible.

Arguments are like playing Jenga knowing that
at any moment, the bricks will topple on you.
All it does, is hurt.

For years I got on board with trying an amicable
relationship but that ship sailed and met an
iceberg.

Happily accepting a backdate of affection from
someone you loved, never clears the emotional
debt owed.

At this point in my life, it doesn't go down easy,
It's like eating a meal without speaking blessing
over the food.

I refuse to feed on scraps, overfilling on
something I shouldn't have had to work so hard
to obtain.

Sometimes I say grace but starve whilst I pick
off the toppings. It's like I'm smacking myself
with a brick just so it goes down.

I've had to understand that I never needed to be
like Oliver, begging just to get a little 'more' of
what I needed.

Satisfied with the unequivocal certainty that
being me was enough to love and show
undiluted adoration.

Nowadays, I refuse to take my needle and thread
to help sow the torn piece of another man's
ripped jean pocket.

Shadow

There are so many of us, boys who grew up with
a shadow for a father.
Their presence is cold on the best of days, and
dark on the rest.
See, there is no refuge.
When you try to express yourself, you sound
like a stooge.
The thing about the boys who grew up with
shadows is, they always feel the cold.
Wearing puffer jackets and night vision goggles
just so they can see.

Those boys then become men who walk around
and exist with an extra layer in case it gets cold
again.
So when I say there are many of us, it means I
recognise a brother who adjusted to seeing in the
dark.
I call out to them - Friend! I see you and I've
journeyed the arctic storms too.
Can I walk alongside you to feel some warmth?

Grapefruit

How do you describe to someone,
That the air often feels poisonous?
And how the thoughts in your mind are maggots,
Nesting on my insecurities.

If I were to describe my mental state on my bad
day, it'd be a grapefruit.

Deceptive in nature.
Bright, warm, and inviting outwardly,
However, internally it feels acidic and sour.
Cut me open with a knife of words,
You'll see my insides spewing out with each
vowel.

Unspoken

My memory is sharp.
And from time to time, it's put to the test.
Versions of events may vary, but I remember the
unspoken.

There is a well of emotions that overflow.
Reminding me of those times, as they are called
into question. I kneel at the mercy seat of those
who prosecute me with my blood on their hands.

Always prepared to crucify me for my latest
indiscretions. They are quick to hurl fragments
of the truth. Tampering with the evidence to fit a
history that favours them.

I begin to look over files in my mind that prove
my innocence.

My body keeps score and testifies with quakes
of anger. There is no denying that trauma
slumbers in my bones.

Triggered by memories that arise,
I belong to a culture that refuses for the guilty
party to be exposed. With my hands tied down,

the plea remains unspoken and the case is
thrown out by the judge.

When my therapist asks me what I'm thinking

When my therapist asks me what I'm thinking?
I say I'm tired of lifting the offenses carried out
in their relationship.
Whether I like it or not, I'm a witness to the
emotional massacres that ensued.

When my therapist asks me what I'm thinking?
I mumble, my eyes are tired of shedding tears at
the scene of the crime. Mourning the spot where
my dreams were ruthlessly assassinated.

When my therapist asks me what I'm thinking?
I grumble, sharing how my emotions have
gotten too heavy for me to contain.
I grow fatigued each day I filter them with the
phrase 'I'm fine'.

When my therapist asks me what I'm thinking?
I whisper, I can't keep going.

Parentification

When I was eight, I could change diapers and
bathe an infant. By twelve, I'd return home from
a day of schooling and think of what to feed the
family. At sixteen, I could run a household
single-handedly whilst co-parenting a child.
I grew up too soon.

As a child of immigrant parents, you step up in
ways that most can't.
It's never their fault.
It takes a village to raise a child, and sometimes
a child has to support a village.
And the children who parented me, helped a
village or two in my childhood.
They grew up too soon.

Inner Child

Let your inner child come out to play.

The world is full of moments where it knocks on
the door situated on memory lane,
Just begging for a chance to play.
Allow yourself out with no curfew or timed
return as the street lights switch on.

Whether it's a smell that takes you back,
A photo of your favourite outfit,
The song you love to sing,
Or dances around the house.
Celebrate with unadulterated happiness.
Your inner child is a reflection of what sets you
alight.

Knock, knock.

Will you come out to play?

Breathe

This is a gentle reminder to breathe.

Have you ever noticed that as humans,
We don't often take a moment to breathe.

This is a gentle reminder to breathe

Our lungs routinely work as a means of survival
but, When was the last time you took a pause,
and drew a breath for pleasure?

This is a gentle reminder to breathe in for four,
hold for four, and out for four.

Selah

An ancient Hebrew word meaning to pause, with an interlude of praise accompanied by instruments.

There are times when music speaks the language of my soul. So every now and then, I sit still and wait for her to choose the soundtrack.

She usually knows what to play.

Selah.

the eldest.

This poem is for the eldest children.

You are the human embodiment of a 30-day free
trial subscribed to by your parents.
Parented with a series of errors and attempts like
guessing a forgotten password.

A well-versed United Nations intercessor
between siblings and parents, in hostile
diplomatic situations.
Building a bridge of communication and
interpreting the linguistic generational discord.

A self-proclaimed conductor in the choir of
relational chaos, and doing it without missing a
note. Allowing voices to be heard amidst the
chorus of confusion.

To the unpaid, overworked, and often
undervalued member of the family.
Your work is seen, acknowledged, and
immeasurably valued. And so are you.

Self Raising

At some point in my life,
I realised I needed to finish raising myself.
Telling me how proud I make myself.
And always having a kind word to say about me,
Never taking my own existence for granted.
Looking at the remarkable job I did,
And be able to relish finishing, raising me.

Goliath

In the past three years, I've overcome.
Wrestled with the beast of depression
Decapitated the three-headed snake I like to call
'SELF'.

Self-doubt, Self-pity, and Self-destruction.
I called myself a victor each time I stepped over
the corpse of my past insecurities and regaled
those who'd listen.

Sharing about my many exploits of healing after
being violated before I even knew how to utter
the word.

I am the victorious, heavy-weight champion of
adversity. Yes, my frame is small compared to
my fellow man but let me assure you.

These bones have battled with enough demons,
dealt with the devil, and been put in a furnace.
There's not a well I've not been pushed down by
a brother or two, and lion's mouths that couldn't
be trapped shut.

Somehow, each time I'm left to die.

I rise up from the grave with a rock and a slingshot.

The next time I face Goliath, I'll aim between the eyes.

Just like fire

I'm just like fire,
I can light a room with my presence.
My voice billows like wildfire smoke.
Within me lies the power to warm your heart or
reduce you to ash.
Snap crackle and pop - I'll make sure you see
me coming.
I'll consume all you give me, leaving a trail
behind.
There's always evidence of my handy work.
Just like fire, don't play with me or you will get
burned.

Love Underground

The Northern Line will always be ours.
Each station along the black line,
Was an exciting breadcrumb trail to your flat.

We shared kisses at Oval,
Strolled side by side around in Clapham
Common,
Our oasis - filled with hipsters, overpriced coffee
shops and homes.

The north star that led us home on Sundays,
Took us through Maida Vale.
It was all one glorious movie that I'd relive all
again.
With you and I, in the lead.
Holding hands like Mary and Tim.

It's as if there are monuments set up in memorial
of the time we spent.
My heart beats fast when I go past Stockwell.
Electric pulses send me off track, with thoughts
speeding back to you.

Nowadays, I avoid taking the northern line.
I often feel my body betrays me.

Priming me for that feeling of ecstasy, only for it to wash away.

The Bad Guy

What if I told you I was the bad guy?
I was the reason why our relationship failed.
Would that bring back the pieces of our shattered
hearts on the ground?
Resuscitate the living memory of our love.
Can it vindicate our love story?

If I made you the punching bag for my
emotions.
Painted you the villain and exhibited you in a
gallery for all to see.
There hangs the woman that did me wrong.
Can it justify the failed fairytale?

Truthfully, ever after ended at the stroke of
midnight.
I fled the scene before the horsemen and
carriage turned to mice and a pumpkin.

I ran from you, but when you returned our
keepsakes,
The ones that chronicled our love affair,
I knew then, that it was the end of our story.

I think I like someone

I think I like someone who likes me.
Since I meet them I've felt so free.
Now I wake up and their face is all I see.
I've fallen so hard, I'm now on one knee.

I think I like someone who likes me.
Sitting in their shade as if they're a tree.
I see how easy it is to rest and simply be.
My heart's emotions are hard to decree.

But I think I like someone who likes me.

Caterpillars and Car Crashes

Suppressing the excitement of knowing you,
Reading your texts with all the right words.

I pull away from the webs you spin about us,
Don't let me dream of us laying on a bed of
roses.

Your replies are like a coin dozer at an arcade,
A flurry of ringing notifications flooding in
makes a melody.

Warning signs appear when I hear them,
Will these feelings end up in a car crash?

In my stomach caterpillars begin to cocoon,
Waiting to sprout wings, transforming into
butterflies.

Daring to love again is like being stuck in a
closet, claustrophobic and strangely warm.

I keep trying to stay down on the see-saw,
But you've not failed in lifting me up.

All I want to do is stay in the shadows,
But your warmth is what I desire to bask in.

One Day

I hope that someday,
I'll wake up to your smile
And the sunlight looking down on my face.
Feeling the warmth from our duvet,
Your arms wrapped around me tight.

I hope that someday,
I'll be brave to love someone like you,
Wearing our love with pride.
Sealing it with a kiss & vow.

I hope that one day,
I'll be blissfully existing in my someday,
every day.

Friendship

The older I get, the more I realise
My friendships are based on me being the
infrastructure that keeps it upright.

When it comes to friendship
I've built a career on pro-bono work.
Volunteering was my strength until I hit
emotional bankruptcy.

The infrastructure of which my friendships rests
is based on the premise of me supporting them.
I've made an art form out of being needed in my
friendships so that I'm never discarded.

Thank you

Shout out to the friends that refuse to speak
about themselves the entire conversation, just to
hear me speak.

I'm not good at making boundaries and
prioritising myself.
Vocalising what I need is not a skill I've honed.
But I've found a handful of people, who are
what I call my hand-railing friends. Walking me
through my emotions, views, and opinions.

Shout out to the friends that refuse to speak
about themselves the entire conversation, just to
hear me speak.

Worthy

The vow of friendship I choose to create with myself, needs to be holy and revered.

Choosing me was the best decision I've ever made. Though it came at the cost of hurting someone else.

My whole world has changed now.
February was the month it dawned on me,
That my worthiness was finally growing roots in the soil of who I am.

www.ingramcontent.com/pod-product-compliance
Lightning Source LLC
LaVergne TN
LVHW010846200726
843508LV00012B/2773